I would like to thank God, my Lord and Savior, for always showing me favor. I would like to thank my twin daughters, Kameron and Kayden for helping me to grow into the woman I am today and being the inspiration for me to write this book; I love you both. Lastly, I would like to thank all my friends and family for believing in me.

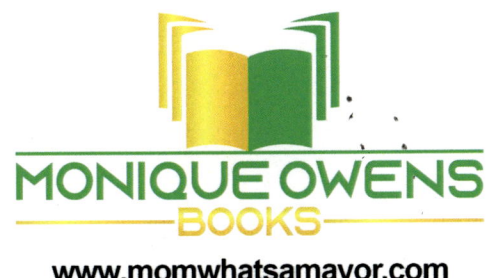

MONIQUE OWENS BOOKS

www.momwhatsamayor.com

CITY HALL

Kameron and Kayden are twin sisters. They just received some exciting news. Their mom was just elected as the first African American mayor of the city of Eastpointe, Michigan. Everyone in the community of Eastpointe was happy that their mom, Monique Owens, was victorious in her election, but Kameron and Kayden were not exactly sure what the job of a mayor was.

6

One day while their mom was at home, Kameron and Kayden asked shyly, "Mom, what's a mayor?" Their mom gave them both a hug. She smiled and said, "I am glad you asked." Their mom had them have a seat next to her as she began to explain what a mayor does, and if you follow along, you can learn too.

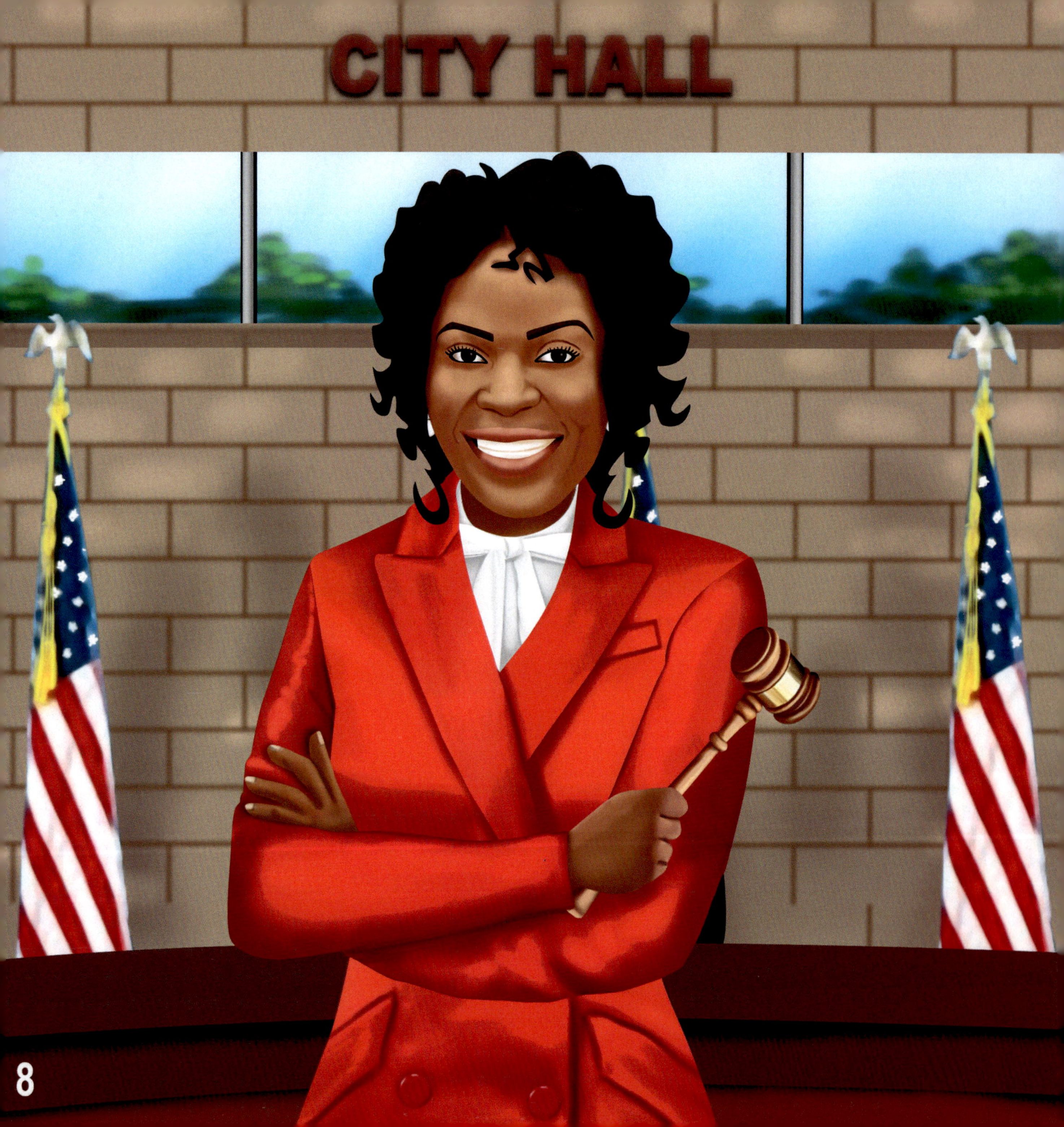
CITY HALL

The mayor is the chief executive officer of a large city or town. Mayors are either elected by the people or appointed by city council. Their terms to serve can consist of 2 to 4 year terms, and some are term limited depending upon the city. Mayors work at city hall alongside the city council to help voice the concerns of the people by making decisions for the betterment of the community.

A mayor pro-tem is a councilmember that has been selected by the city council to serve in the absence of the mayor temporarily until they return.

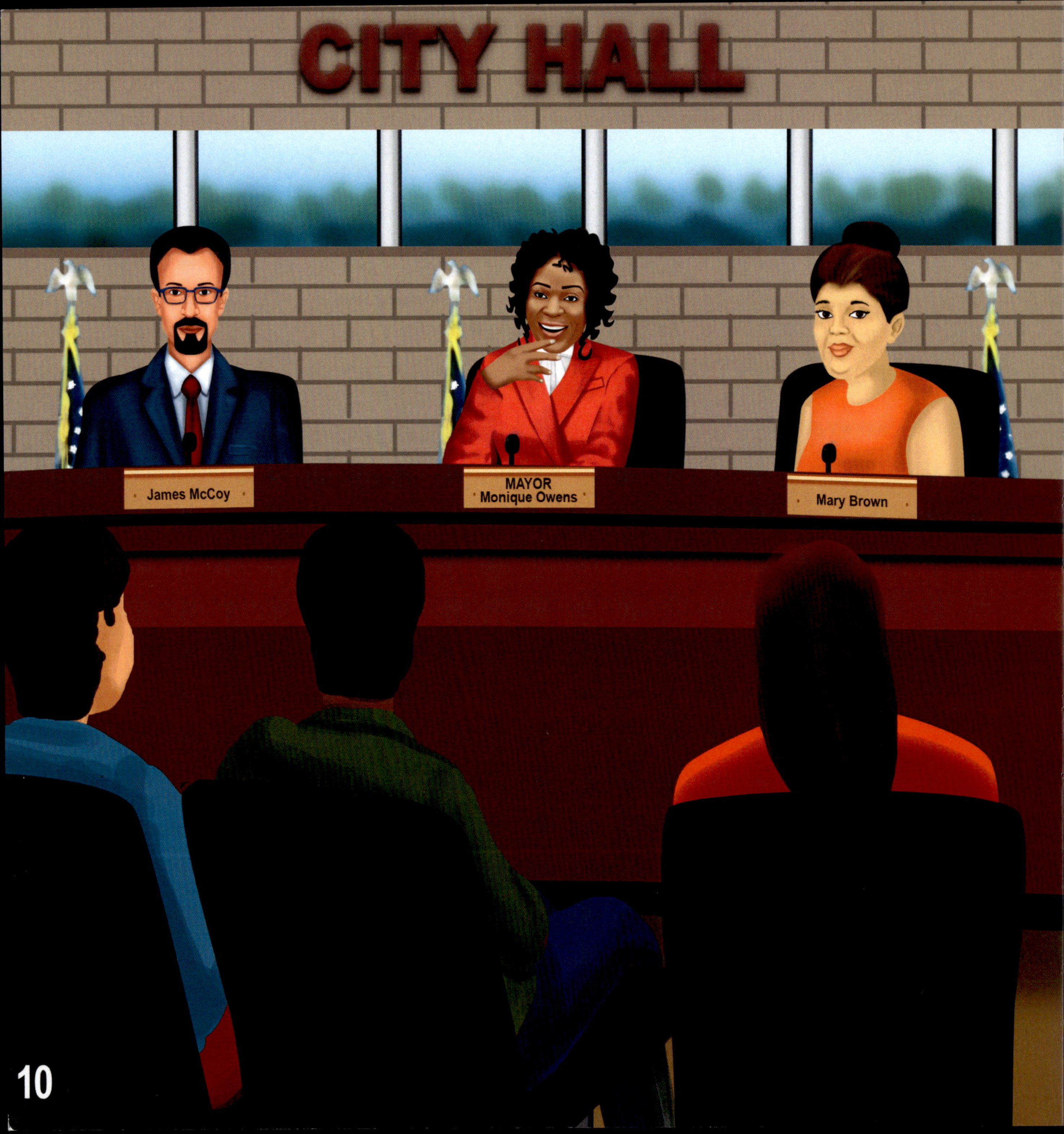
CITY HALL
James McCoy
MAYOR
Monique Owens
Mary Brown

A mayor can come in two forms of government. Unlimited mayor form and limited mayor form of government. The unlimited mayor form of government has no city manager, is usually in larger cities, and they work full-time. The mayor is the head administrator of staff and is a part of the legislative body. The unlimited mayor is the only person who can veto a law-making decision.

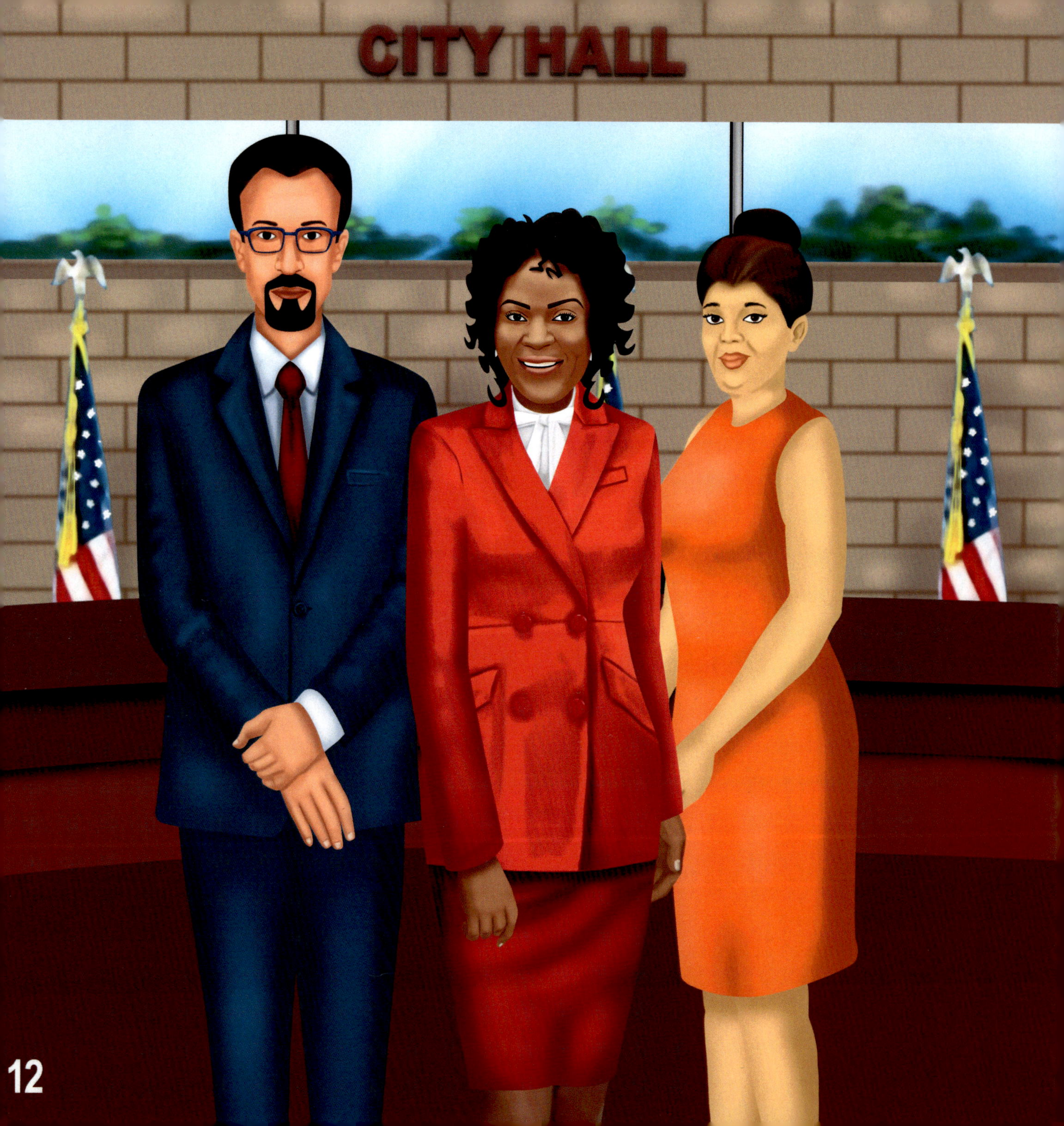
CITY HALL

Another form is limited mayor form of government, which has a city manager. The city manager works to support the mayor and city council along with the department directors. The mayor is a part of the city council, and together they work part-time to manage the budget, improve the city's streets, and create laws. The limited mayor form cannot veto a decision.

CERTIFICATE of Outstanding Achievement
Awarded to
Mayor Monique Owens
CERTIFICATE of Appreciation
Awarded to
Mayor Monique Owens
City Charter

The city charter defines the organization, procedures and powers of a city. It is the most important legal document. It assists the mayor and city council with their responsibilities and helps the residents understand the laws and functions of government in their city or town. The laws can always be amended, changed, or newly created by city council or by the vote of the residents.

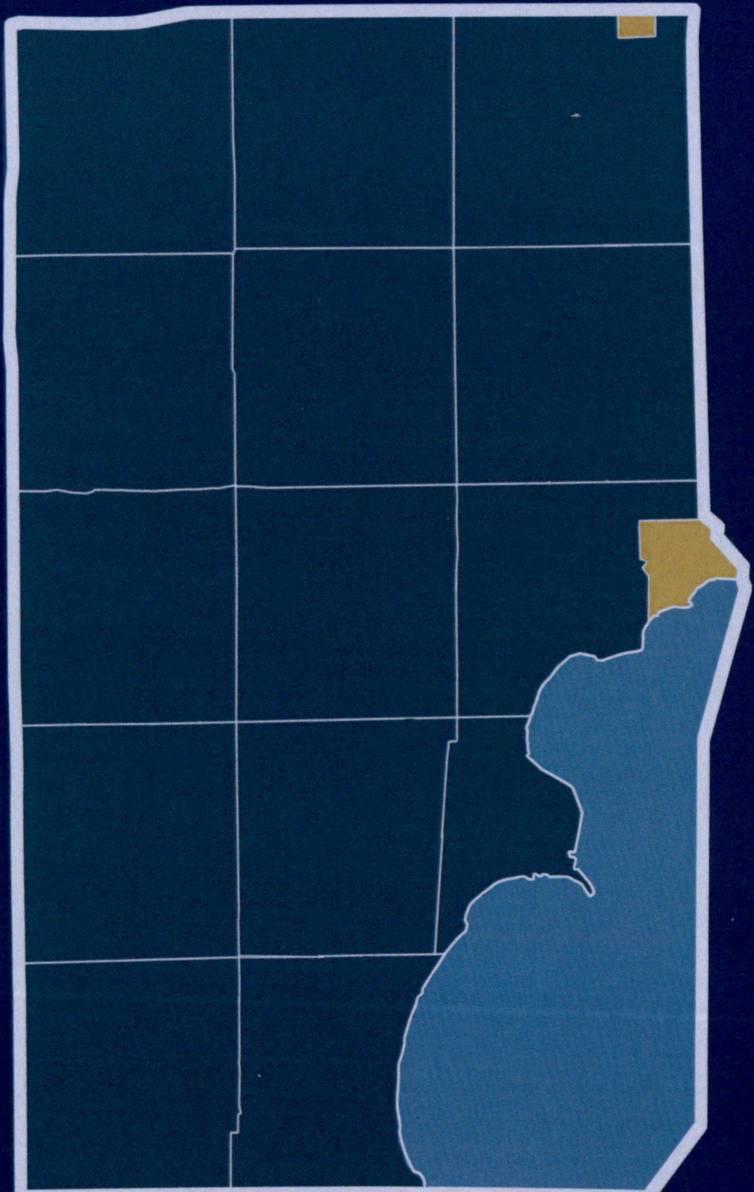

A member of city council may serve the city at large or in districts depending upon the charter of the city. If a councilmember serves a city at large, they must serve the city as a whole. If they are over a district area, they must lead under that district. No matter if it's representing the city at large or at a district level, a council person's job is for the betterment of the entire city.

18

The mayor and city council also conduct council meetings. The council meetings openly allow the mayor and city council to vote on what laws to pass, important matters to address and to hear what the issues and concerns are from the public to better serve them.

20

A mayor also takes part in handling contracts and contractors of the city. Contractors do private work for cities such as landscaping, snow plowing, and construction, which are just a few of the many different contracting jobs in a town.

22

One of the most important jobs of a mayor and city council is to help prepare the yearly budget. The budget is a sum of money, mainly taxpayer money, that is used to run the city to make sure that city workers are paid, roads are fixed, and parks are in good condition so that residents have a better quality of life.

24

Mayors can have fun too! They are the ambassadors of the city. They walk in parades and attend ribbon cuttings to show support to new businesses in the community.

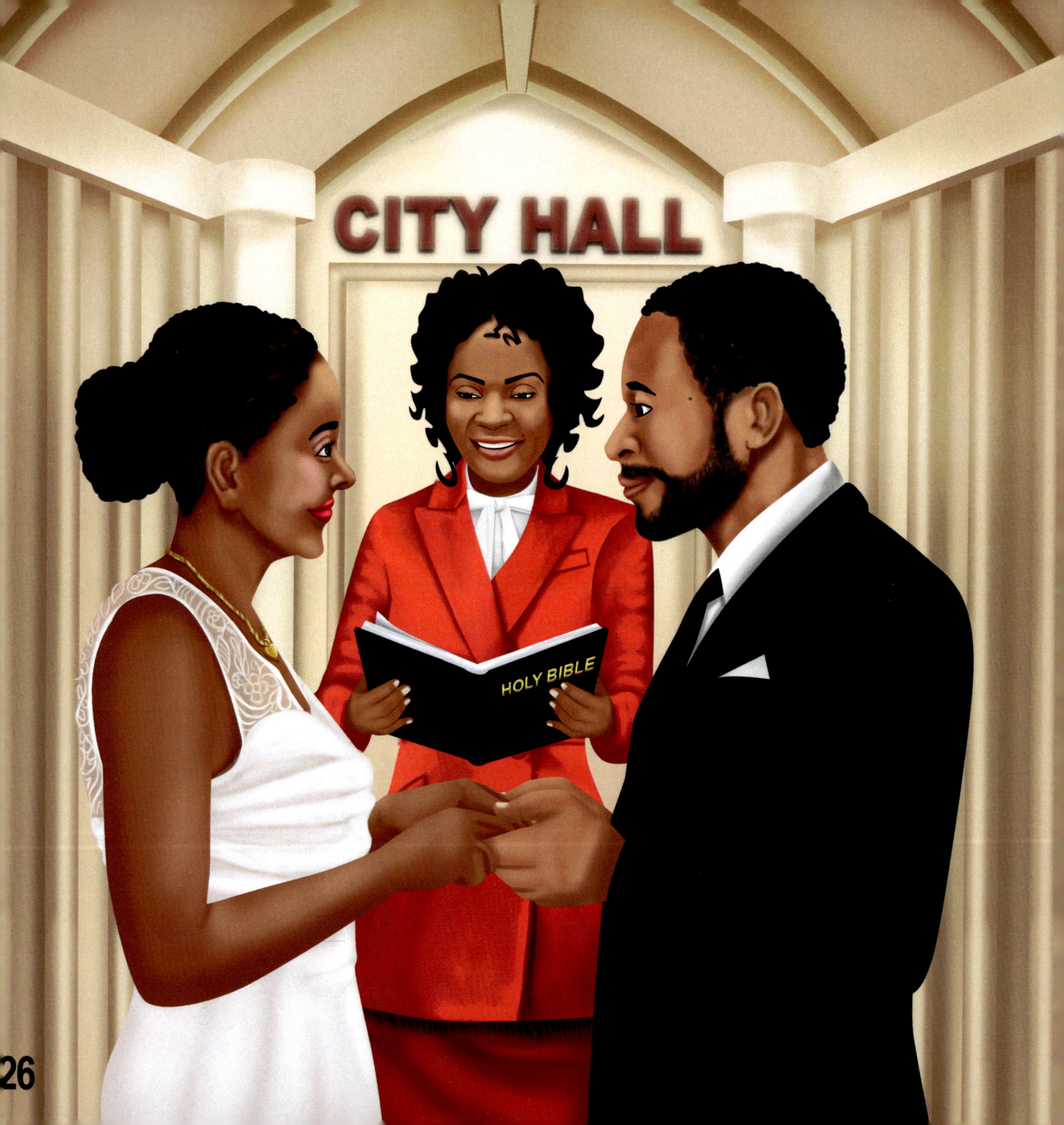
CITY HALL
HOLY BIBLE

They represent the people by supporting businesses, attending community events, performing marriage ceremonies, and adopting proclamations that brings the community together.

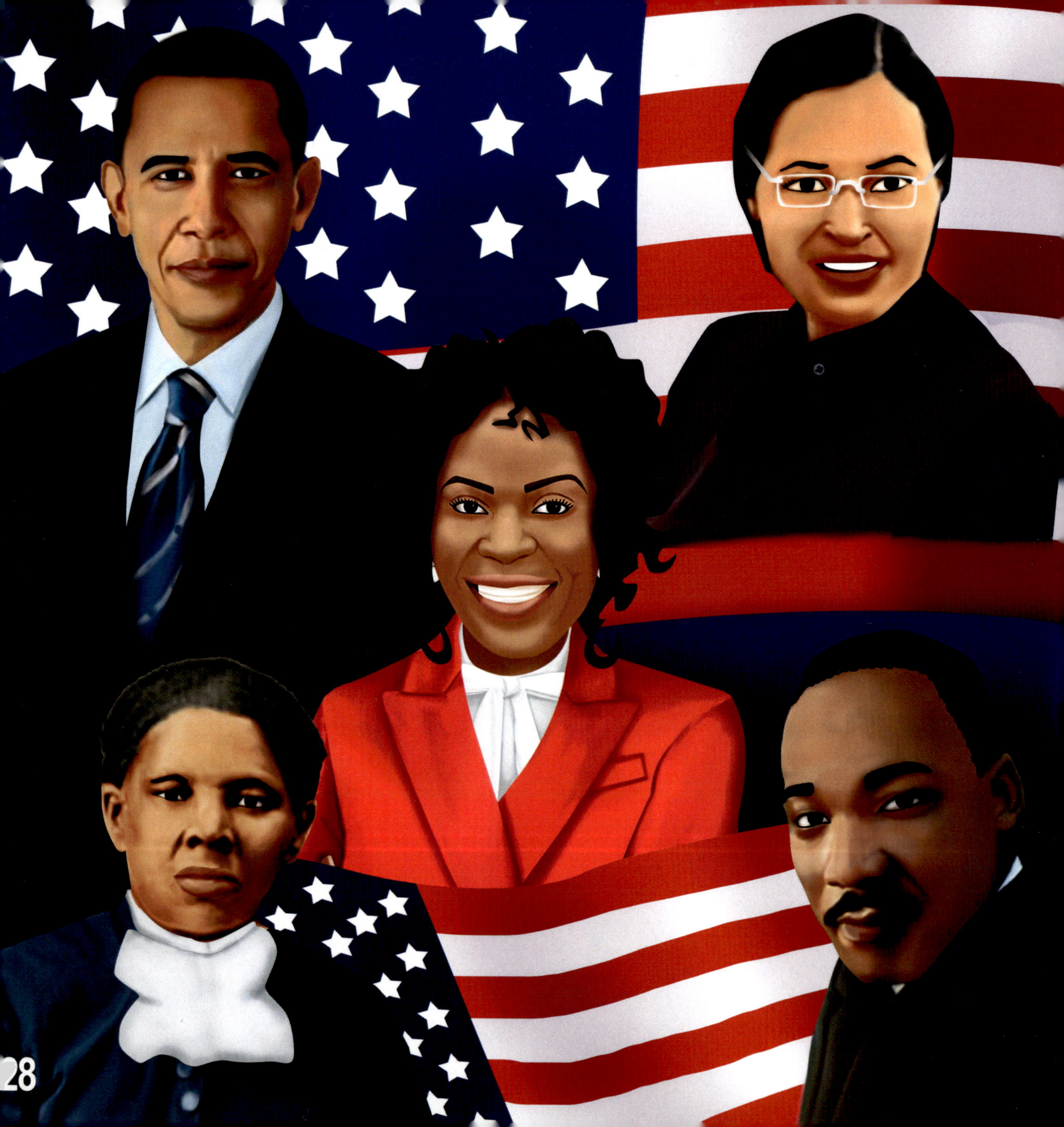

Their mom finished by saying, "And that's the many jobs of a mayor." By the time the twins' mom had finished telling them what a mayor did, they were so excited they couldn't wait to tell all their friends at school the next day. Kayden asked, "Mom, why did everyone say you made history?" Their mom explained that she was the first African American to become the Mayor of Eastpointe, Michigan, and that anytime someone is the first at anything, they make a mark on the world as a history maker.

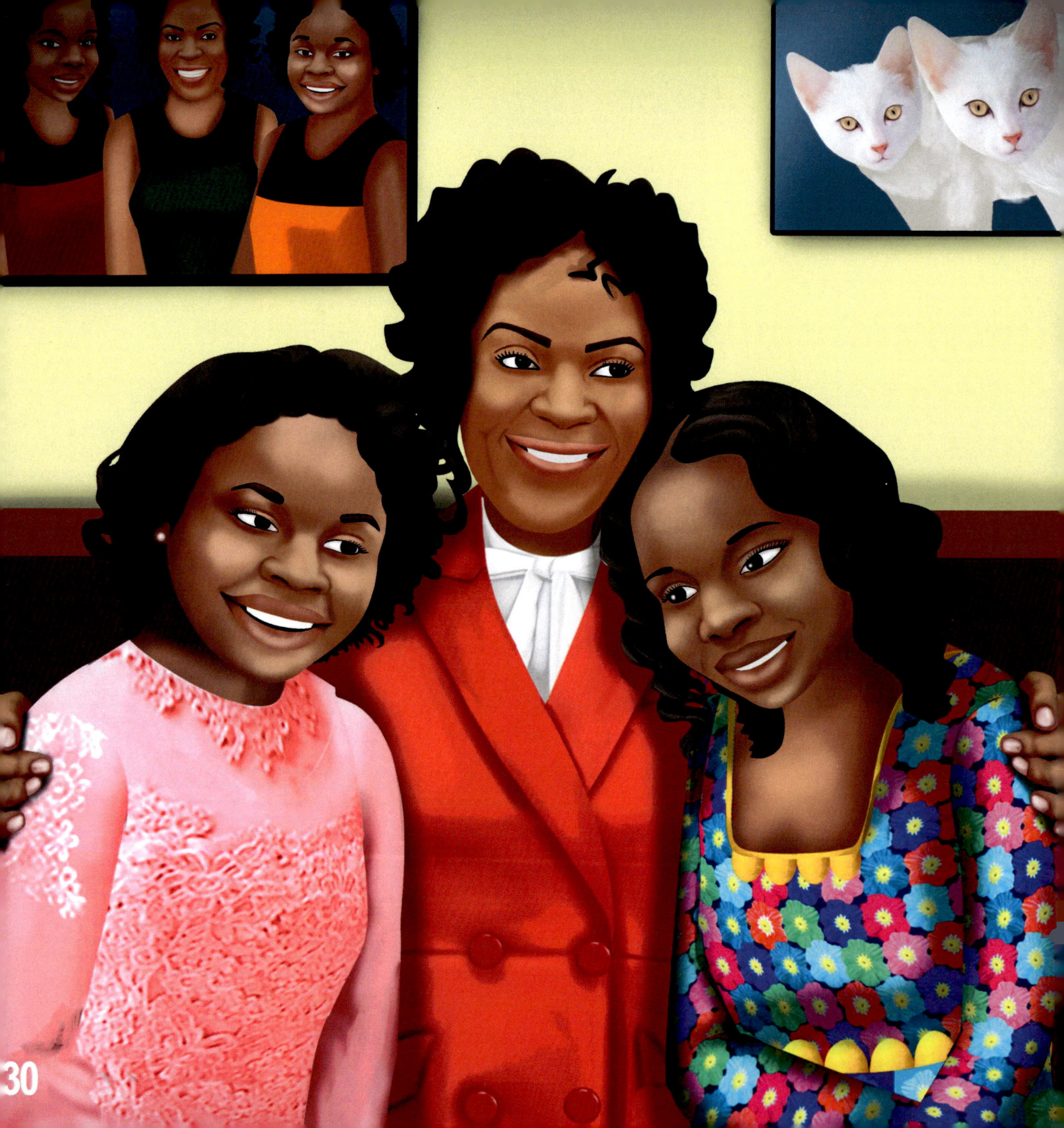

The twins both smiled when they heard this. Kameron asked, "Mom, you know what our favorite part of your job is?"

Their Mom replied, "No, you tell me."

The twins both looked at each other, smiled and said, "Being our mom".

32

Steps in Becoming A Mayor

1. Go to your local clerk's office at city hall for a copy of petitions.

2. Get your petitions signed by registered voters in that city or town.

3. Once you have your list of registered voters, return it to the clerks' office to get each registered voter's name approved.

| James McCoy | MAYOR Monique Owens |

4. Once approved, you become a candidate on the ballot.

5. Once you are on the ballot, it's now time for you to get out and get votes to be elected and run a successful campaign and win.

6. Lastly, you can also be appointed as a councilmember by the city council without being elected by the people.

Test Your Skills

What is a mayor?

A) An individual that eats pizza
B) An individual that helps the community
C) An individual that looks at cartoons
D) The chief executive of the city
E) All of the above

What is a councilmember?

A) An individual who helps the community
B) An individual who looks at cartoons
C) A legislative member of a group in a city
D) A legislator who creates laws
E) All of the above

What is a mayor pro-tem?

A) A chef
B) A member of city council
C) A lawmaker
D) Someone who helps the mayor when they are absent
E) B, C, and D

What is a city charter?

A) A document
B) A guide that helps the community understand the rules of a city
C) A coloring book
D) A guide for the mayor and city council
E) A, B and D

The type of jobs contractors do.

A) Landscaping
B) Snowplowing
C) Make Popsicles
D) Chase Cats
E) Both A and B

What powers does an unlimited mayor have that a limited mayor does not have?

A) They can veto a law
B) They can hire administration
C) They can help create new laws
D) Sign contracts for city businesses
E) Both A and B

What is a budget?

A) A monthly / yearly sum of money
B) A car rental place
C) Funds that help pay for city roads and parks
D) Funds that help pay city employees
E) A, C and D

How can you become a mayor or councilmember?

A) By being elected by the people
B) By drinking slushies
C) By being appointed by city council members
D) By respecting others and helping your community
E) A, C, and D

Answers: If you answered E for all the questions, you were right! Great job!

Words To Know So You Can Grow

Ambassador (am-bass-si-door): an authorized representative or messenger

Appoint (a-point): to hire or decide

Ballot (bal-ut): a document used to vote for something or someone in writing or by marking

Budget (bud-jit): a yearly sum of money used to run a city or town

Candidate (can-di-date): a person who applies to be considered for something

Ceremonies (ser-i-mo-knees): a special occasion or celebration of something

Citizen (Sit-i-zen): someone born in or has moved to the United States from another country

City (Sit-tee): a settlement or place with defined boundaries that provides citizens with government services

City charter: a document that directs the council on the responsibilities of a city and helps residents understand the laws within their city

City council (cown-cil): the legislative body of a city that help make laws for a city or town

City hall: the main administrative building that houses the government body and its city employees

City manager (man-knee-jer): a person employed by an elected council to assist in the administration of city government

Clerk's office (cl-irk)(aw-fuss): a public officer charged with recording the official proceedings and vital statistics of a city

Construction (con-struc-shun): a sculpture that is put together out of separate pieces of materials

Contractor: one that contracts to perform work or provide supplies

Contract: an agreement or promise that is legal between a person or persons to do something or not to do something (can be written or verbal)

Council meetings: located at city hall, where a city council makes decisions and residents can voice their concerns

Councilmember (cown-cil): a member of a group of legislators that represent a city or town

District/Ward (diss-stric-t): a city divided into areas for representation and administrative purposes

Elect (e-lekt): to vote by choosing someone to lead or to hold public office

Election (e-lec-shun): a way to determine a candidate to a form of government

Gavel (gav-ul): a mallet, small in size, that is used to call for order or attention by a mayor, judge, auctioneer, or someone that is the chair of a meeting

Government (guv-er-ment): authoritative direction or control, the office, a function of governing

Landscaping (land-skap-ing): a picture representing a view of natural inland scenery

Law (l-ah-w): A set of rules in a state or country that citizens must obey

Legislator (le-ji-sley-tor): one that makes laws, especially for a political unit

Local (lo-coal): primarily serving the needs of a particular district

Mayor (may-your): the chief executive of a city or town of a municipal government that makes decisions on behalf of a city or town

Mayor-Pro Tem: a councilperson selected by city council to temporarily serve in the absence of the mayor

Municipal government (mu-ni-see-pole): a small city or town that is ran by a body of local legislative leaders

Petitions (pi-ti-shun): a document that requires a signature asking a request of something

Proclamation (pro-cla-may-shun): an official public document and announcement usually issued by the mayor to show honor for a specific purpose or worthy cause

Registered voter(re-ji-stirred): a person who is eligible to vote in the United States

Resident (re-zi-dent): a person who resides in a location for an extended period

Snow plowing: a device used for clearing away snow

Tax: a sum of money paid to the government

Taxpayer: a business entity or someone who pays taxes to the government

Term: a length of time in which one who is elected or appointed can serve

Veto (vee-toe): to dismiss or reject

Monique Owens

Photography by: Derek Dandridge

ABOUT THE AUTHOR

Monique Owens is what many identify as a trailblazer. Setting the standard high as an influential leader with poise, class, and historical determination, Monique Owens continues to show what excellence looks like. She was born in Detroit, Michigan on February 21,1984, and although she was considered gifted and inquisitive by her teachers, at the age of 34 years old was when her historic journey began. Monique Owens was elected in 2017 as Eastpointe's First African American councilmember. In 2019, only two years in her term, she decided to run for mayor and became Eastpointe's first African American and youngest mayor to hold office in Macomb County's history.

In 2020, She was selected to attend the Bloomberg Harvard Leadership Initiative that included over 40 mayors worldwide. This initiative gives mayors the resources to become more effective leaders, instructed by the top educators from all over the United States. In addition, she was awarded a scholarship by the Taubman Foundation and was hand-selected by Southeast Michigan Council of Governments, to attend the John F. Kennedy School for Executive Leaders at Harvard University in Cambridge, MA.

In 2021, She received the "Women of Excellence Award" from the Michigan Chronicle for her leadership in her community and paving the way for future leaders. She has been highlighted on several national platforms including MSNBC and Wallstreet Journal. She started Owens Political Consulting Firm to help future candidates running for office to be strategic in planning a more successful campaign focusing on minority groups to increase diversity within our political system.

Her fight for social justice in creating equality across the board started in her work as a Wayne County Deputy Sheriff. While serving as an officer she received her Bachelor's Degree in Political Science from Madonna University. Monique realized that she wanted to do more than just enforce the law, but create laws that would ensure a better quality of life for all people.

Monique Owens' talents doesn't stop there. As a former comedian she connected with the world by using humor to steer joy. She won an audition with the famous "Showtime At The Apollo", which led her to start her own talent agency called "Naturally Funny Talent Agency" that gave a platform for up and coming comedians to showcase their talents.